U.S. PRESIDENTS

MYTHS OR FACTS?

MYTHS AND FACTS ABOUT THOMAS JEFFERSON

EZRA E. KNOPP

PowerKiDS press

Published in 2024 by The Rosen Publishing Group, Inc.
2544 Clinton Street, Buffalo, NY 14224

First Edition

Editor: Greg Roza
Book Design: Michael Flynn

Photo Credits: Cover Werkat/Shutterstock.com; (series background) Azamatovic/Shutterstock.com; p. 5 eurobanks/Shutterstock.com; p. 7 courtesy of the Library of Congress; p. 9 https://commons.wikimedia.org/wiki/File:Megalonyx_wheatleyi_skeleton_%26_restoration.jpg; p. 11 Richard Hood/Shutterstock.com; p. 13 Stokkete/Shutterstock.com; p. 15 https://commons.wikimedia.org/wiki/File:Lewis_and_clark-expedition.jpg; p. 17 courtesy of the Smithsonian Institution; p. 19 elisank79/Shutterstock.com; p. 20 https://commons.wikimedia.org/wiki/File%3A02_Thomas_Jefferson_3x4.jpg.

Cataloging-in-Publication Data

Names: Knopp, Ezra E.
Title: Myths and facts about Thomas Jefferson / Ezra E. Knopp.
Description: New York : Powerkids Press, 2024. | Series: U.S. Presidents: myths or facts? | Includes glossary and index.
Identifiers: ISBN 9781499444162 (pbk.) | ISBN 9781499444179 (library bound) | ISBN 9781499444186 (ebook)
Subjects: LCSH: Jefferson, Thomas, 1743-1826–Juvenile literature. | Presidents–United States–Biography–Juvenile literature. | United States–History–Errors, inventions, etc.–Juvenile literature.
Classification: LCC E332.79 K64 2024 | DDC 973.4'6092–dc23

Manufactured in the United States of America

CPSIA Compliance Information: Batch #CWPK24. For Further Information contact Rosen Publishing at 1-800-237-9932.

CONTENTS

A WEALTHY UPBRINGING

Thomas Jefferson was born April 13, 1743, near Charleston, Virginia. His father, Peter, was a wealthy **plantation** owner. His mother, Jane, was a member of the wealthy Randolph family. Thomas was the third of 10 children and the oldest boy.

Growing up in a world of wealth and privilege, Jefferson was allowed to roam his father's land at will. He took a great early interest in the natural world. When Jefferson was 14, however, his father died. Thomas inherited his father's land in the Virginia colony—about 5,000 acres (2,023 ha)!

IT'S A FACT!

JEFFERSON IS A CELEBRATED FIGURE IN THE FIGHT FOR AMERICAN INDEPENDENCE, BUT HIS **LEGACY** HAS BEEN HARMED BECAUSE OF HIS USE OF ENSLAVED PEOPLE. HIS FAMILY'S PLANTATION USED ENSLAVED LABOR, AND HE CONTINUED TO ENSLAVE PEOPLE FOR THE REST OF HIS LIFE.

IN 1768, JEFFERSON HAD AN AREA OF LAND AT THE TOP OF A HILL CLEARED TO BUILD A HOME, WHICH HE NAMED MONTICELLO (ITALIAN FOR "LITTLE MOUNTAIN"). JEFFERSON DESIGNED THE HOME AND SURROUNDING GARDENS, AND HE WOULD CONTINUE TO UPDATE THE HOUSE FOR MOST OF HIS LIFE.

MYTH OR FACT?

JEFFERSON WAS A POOR STUDENT.

MYTH

From an early age, Jefferson enjoyed reading and playing the violin. When he was just nine years old, he began learning Latin and Greek from a local scholar. In the following years, Jefferson also studied literature and mathematics.

In 1760, Jefferson began attending the College of William and Mary in Williamsburg, Virginia. Reports say that he spent most of the day reading, studying, and practicing the violin. He met several **mentors** there. William Small was a teacher of mathematics and science. George Wythe was a talented legal scholar.

IT'S A FACT!

JEFFERSON'S KNOWLEDGE OF LITERATURE, LANGUAGES, AND HISTORY HELPED HIM DRAFT THE DECLARATION OF INDEPENDENCE, ONE OF THE MOST IMPORTANT DOCUMENTS IN U.S. HISTORY. IT ALSO HELPED HIM REACH THE OFFICE OF PRESIDENT.

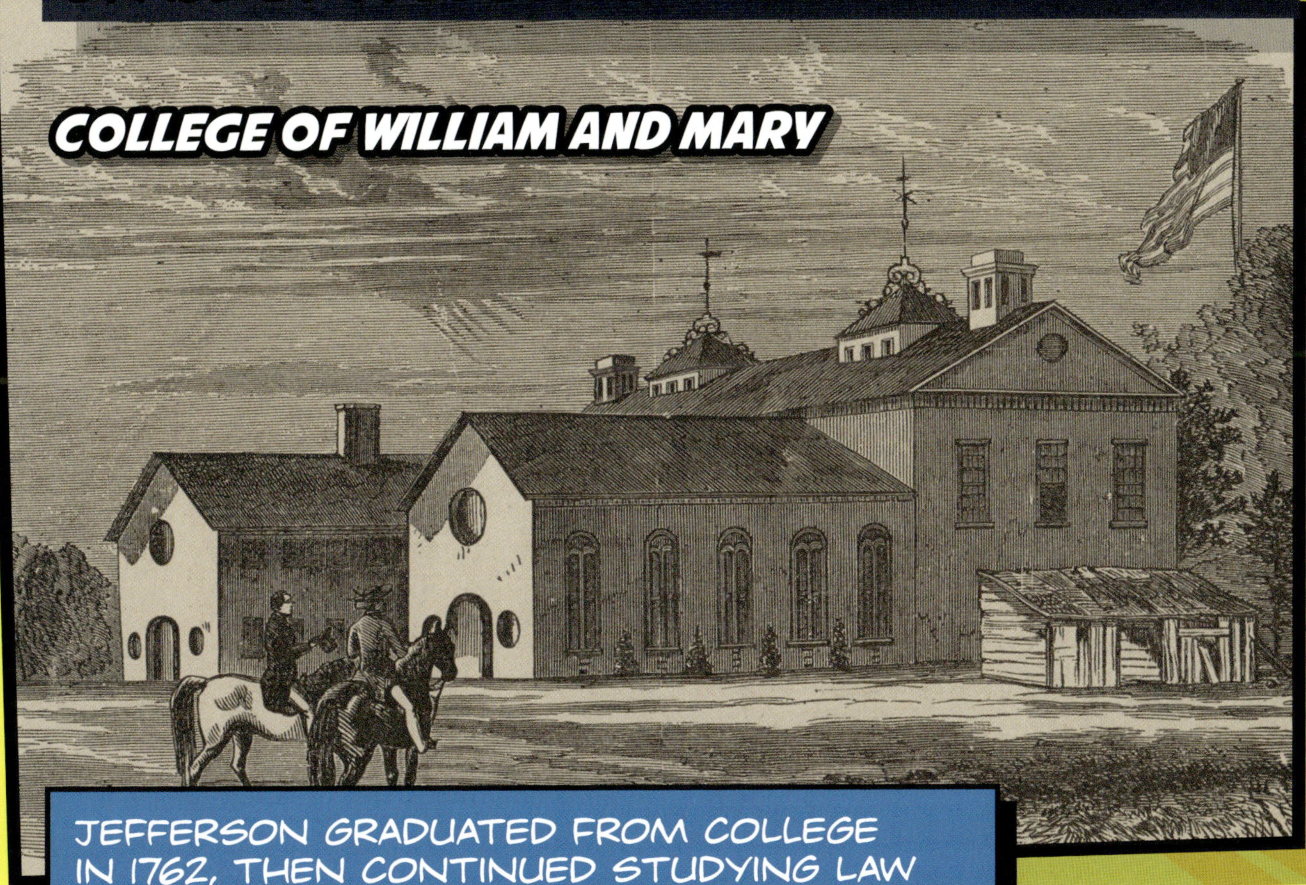

JEFFERSON GRADUATED FROM COLLEGE IN 1762, THEN CONTINUED STUDYING LAW UNDER WYTHE. HE BEGAN WORKING AS A LAWYER IN 1767.

CRAVING KNOWLEDGE

MYTH OR FACT?

JEFFERSON HAD A BONE ROOM IN THE WHITE HOUSE.

FACT

The natural world was a source of interest for Jefferson for all of his life. He collected numerous **minerals**, metals, **fossils**, and bones. He was particularly interested in the remains of mastodons that once roamed North America. He even displayed them in the White House.

Jefferson received bones that were found in a cave in West Virginia. He decided that they belonged to a huge mammal with sharp claws. He named this creature *Megalonyx* (Greek for "great claw"). Jefferson though that mastodons and *Megalonyx* still existed, but we now know that they were both **extinct** by this time.

JEFFERSON GUESSED THAT *MEGALONYX* WAS A HUGE LION. HOWEVER, IT WAS ACTUALLY THE REMAINS OF AN ANIMAL RELATED TO SLOTHS. SCIENTISTS HONORED JEFFERSON BY NAMING THE EXTINCT GIANT SLOTH AFTER HIM: *MEGALONYX JEFFERSONII*.

MYTH OR FACT?

JEFFERSON INTRODUCED SOME OF AMERICANS' FAVORITE FOODS TO THE UNITED STATES.

MYTH

Jefferson was an inventor and **innovator**. He invented a movable book stand that could hold multiple books. He may have improved several other inventions, such as the swivel chair and the dumbwaiter, a type of small elevator.

Some myths about Jefferson say he introduced certain foods to the Unites States, including ice cream, mac and cheese, and french fries. While these stories aren't true, it is true that Jefferson helped make these foods popular. Recipes for them appear in Jefferson's notes.

IT'S A FACT!

AT THE TIME, MANY PEOPLE BELIEVED TOMATOES WERE POISONOUS. JEFFERSON, HOWEVER, GREW THEM AT MONTICELLO AND ENJOYED EATING THEM RAW.

YOU CAN STILL VISIT THE BEAUTIFUL GARDENS OF MONTICELLO TODAY!

A LIFE IN POLITICS MYTH OR FACT?

AS SECRETARY OF STATE UNDER GEORGE WASHINGTON, JEFFERSON TRIED TO BRING THE METRIC SYSTEM TO THE UNITED STATES.

FACT

After the end of the American Revolution, there were several methods of measurement used in the United States. This caused problems. Jefferson suggested that the metric system, used in France, would be the perfect solution. However, Congress stalled on the idea, and the system was never adopted.

There's a dramatic addition to this story. In 1793, French scientist Joseph Dombey was bringing information on the metric system to the United States for Jefferson. However, Dombey's ship was attacked by pirates! The information never made it to Jefferson, but he was already convinced about it anyway.

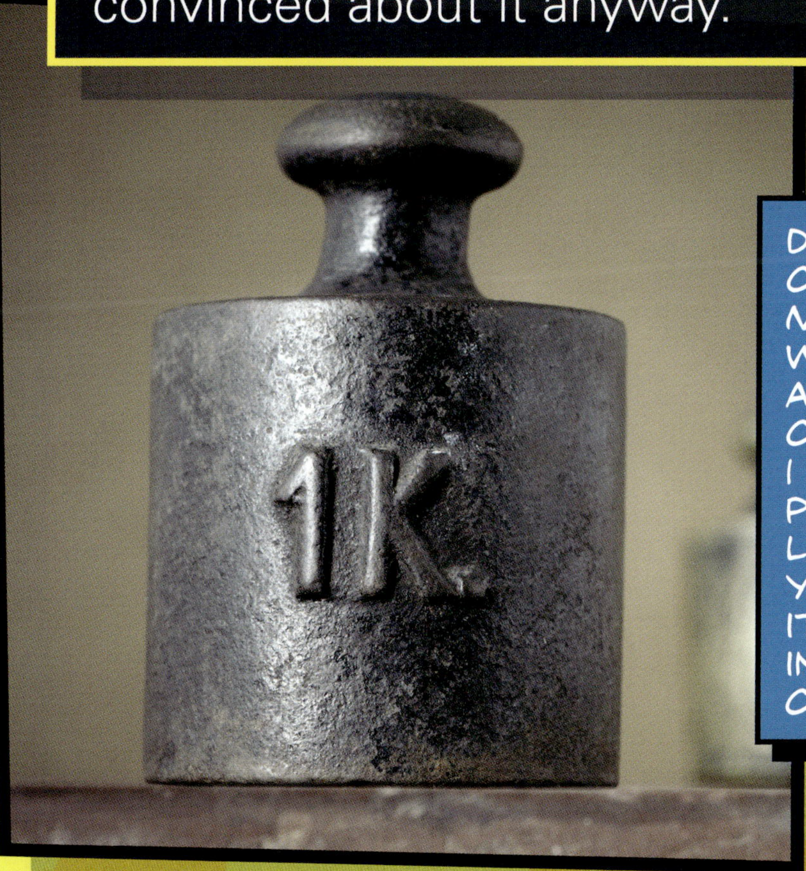

DOMBEY WAS CARRYING A SMALL METAL **CYLINDER** WITH A HANDLE AT THE TOP. THIS CYLINDER WEIGHED 1 KILOGRAM (2.2 POUNDS). IT WAS LOST FOR MANY YEARS UNTIL IT TURNED UP IN A PERSONAL COLLECTION IN 1954.

MYTH OR FACT?

DURING HIS FIRST TERM AS PRESIDENT, JEFFERSON DOUBLED THE SIZE OF THE UNITED STATES.

FACT

In 1803, Jefferson made the greatest land purchase in history: the Louisiana Territory. The area of this territory was nearly 830,000 square miles (2,149,690 sq km). The United States paid France $15 million, which is about four cents per acre! This purchase effectively doubled the size of the country.

Jefferson put together a team of explorers known as the Corps of Discovery. This **expedition**, led by Meriwether Lewis and William Clark, lasted about two years. The expedition provided information about wildlife, rivers, geological features, Native groups, and more.

IT'S A FACT!

THE CORPS OF DISCOVERY SENT **SPECIMENS** BACK TO JEFFERSON IN WASHINGTON, D.C. THESE ITEMS INCLUDED FOSSILS, PLANTS, AND EVEN LIVE ANIMALS. JEFFERSON PUT SOME OF THE PLANTS IN HIS GARDENS AT MONTICELLO.

SACAGAWEA, A MEMBER OF THE SHOSHONE PEOPLE, WAS PERHAPS THE MOST FAMOUS PERSON TRAVELING WITH THE CORPS OF DISCOVERY. SHE GUIDED THEM WEST, AND SHE SPOKE WITH NATIVE AMERICAN GROUPS THE CORPS MET ALONG THE WAY.

POST-PRESIDENCY MYTH OR FACT?

JEFFERSON WROTE HIS OWN VERSION OF THE CHRISTIAN BIBLE.

FACT

As a scholar and a Christian, Jefferson felt the **supernatural** elements included in the Bible clouded the true teachings of Jesus Christ. Jefferson used a razor blade to cut out parts of the New Testament (the part of the Bible that tells the story of Jesus's life). He then pasted the words into a new order, leaving out the supernatural elements.

Today, Jefferson's **version** is known as the Jefferson Bible. It is 84 pages long and made up of two volumes.

ALTHOUGH JEFFERSON HAD MENTIONED HIS VERSION OF THE BIBLE TO PEOPLE, HE NEVER SHARED IT WITH ANYONE ELSE. THE FIRST PUBLISHED VERSION WAS NOT AVAILABLE TO THE PUBLIC UNTIL 1904.

MYTH OR FACT?

JEFFERSON WAS VERY GOOD WITH MONEY.

MYTH

Many reports show that Jefferson was in **debt** for most of his life. Before the Revolutionary War, Jefferson fell into debt for several reasons. He **inherited** a large debt when his father-in-law, John Wayles, died in 1774.

Jefferson owned a large plantation, but he wasn't the best at managing it. In addition to that, he often spent large amounts of money on building Monticello and filling it with paintings, furniture, wine, and more. In 1826, Jefferson owed more than $107,000.

IT'S A FACT!

DURING THE WAR OF 1812, THE BRITISH BURNED THE U.S. CAPITOL AND THE LIBRARY OF CONGRESS. IN 1815, TO HELP PAY SOME OF HIS DEBTS, JEFFERSON SOLD HIS PERSONAL LIBRARY TO THE LIBRARY OF CONGRESS FOR $23,950. THIS INCLUDED ABOUT 6,700 BOOKS!

IN RECENT YEARS, THE LIBRARY OF CONGRESS HAS DISPLAYED A RECREATION OF JEFFERSON'S LIBRARY THAT WAS SOLD TO CONGRESS.

Shortly after Jefferson died on July 4, 1826, his family held a sale that included nearly everything inside Monticello. However, the debt Jefferson created during his life wasn't paid off for another 50 years, until his grandson, Thomas Jefferson Randolph, finished paying it.

It's true that Jefferson's legacy was harmed by his own actions. However, it's hard to deny that he was devoted to spreading democracy around the world. Without Jefferson, American independence may have never happened.

JEFFERSON'S TIMELINE

APRIL 13, 1743	THOMAS JEFFERSON IS BORN.
1757	JEFFERSON'S FATHER, PETER, DIES. JEFFERSON INHERITS PETER'S PLANTATION.
1760–1762	JEFFERSON ATTENDS THE COLLEGE OF WILLIAM AND MARY.
1762	JEFFERSON BEGINS TO STUDY LAW UNDER GEORGE WYTHE.
1772	HE MARRIES MARTHA WAYLES SKELTON.
1776	HE WRITES THE DECLARATION OF INDEPENDENCE.
1779–1781	HE SERVES AS GOVERNOR OF VIRGINIA.
1790–1793	HE SERVES AS THE FIRST SECRETARY OF STATE OF THE UNITED STATES.
1797–1801	HE SERVES UNDER JOHN ADAMS AS THE SECOND U.S. VICE PRESIDENT.
1801–1809	HE SERVES AS THE THIRD U.S. PRESIDENT.
1817	HE FOUNDS THE UNIVERSITY OF VIRGINIA.
JULY 4, 1826	JEFFERSON DIES AT MONTICELLO.

GLOSSARY

cylinder: A solid object shaped like a tube.

debt: Money owed to someone else.

expedition: A journey or trip undertaken for a specific purpose, such as exploring an area.

extinct: No longer alive.

fossil: Marks and remains left behind by ancient plants and animals.

inherit: To get something, such money or land, after someone dies and leaves it to you.

innovator: Someone who improves upon the plans or products of others.

legacy: Something that comes from someone in the past.

mentor: Someone who teaches, gives guidance, or gives advice to someone, especially a less experienced person.

mineral: A naturally occurring solid substance that's not of plant or animal origin.

plantation: An agricultural estate, often worked by enslaved people.

specimen: A part or a single thing (such as a bug or animal) that shows what the whole group is like.

supernatural: Unable to be explained by science or the laws of nature.

version: A form of something that is different from the ones that came before it.

FOR MORE INFORMATION

BOOKS

Harrison, Wag. *The Presidents Did What?* Richmond, VA: Belle Isle Books, 2021.

London, Martha. *Thomas Jefferson.* Mendota Heights, MN: North Star Editions, 2023.

Rosenstock, Barb. *Thomas Jefferson Builds a Library.* Honesdale, PA: Calkins Creek Books, 2023.

WEBSITES

Biography: President Thomas Jefferson
www.ducksters.com/biography/uspresidents/thomasjefferson.php
Learn much more about Thomas Jefferson from this detailed website.

Monticello
www.monticello.org
Visit the official website for Jefferson's home, Monticello, to learn more about the building, the gardens, how to visit, and much more.

Publisher's note to educators and parents: Our editors have carefully reviewed these websites to ensure that they are suitable for students. Many websites change frequently, however, and we cannot guarantee that a site's future contents will continue to meet our high standards of quality and educational value. Be advised that students should be closely supervised whenever they access the internet.

INDEX